Original title:
An Orchid's Ode

Copyright © 2025 Creative Arts Management OÜ
All rights reserved.

Author: Charles Whitfield
ISBN HARDBACK: 978-1-80581-845-8
ISBN PAPERBACK: 978-1-80581-372-9
ISBN EBOOK: 978-1-80581-845-8

A Melody of Color and Form

Petals dance with vibrant glee,
Colors clash, quite whimsically.
Leaves debate on who looks best,
Nature's fashion—what a jest!

Stems sway gently, like a tune,
Roses envy how they bloom!
Daisies giggle, tulips smile,
Oh, let's celebrate in style!

Chasing Shadows in Blooming Moments

A bumblebee hums tunes of cheer,
While sunflowers strut—look here, we're near!
Butterflies argue who flies the best,
In this garden, they're all guests!

Petals petulant, waving high,
"I'm the priciest!" one might cry.
But laughter echoes 'neath the trees,
Even weeds join in, if you please!

The Stillness of Blossoming Time

At dawn they wake, with sleepy grins,
Whispers of dew where the day begins.
"What's the rush?" the daisies plead,
"Let's lounge around, take a leisurely lead!"

Tulip tumbles, slips with flair,
While violets gossip, unaware.
The sun's a tease, just peeks and hides,
In stillness, their comedy abides!

Essence of the Unseen

In the garden, secrets bloom,
Unseen giggles fill the room.
Roots chuckle underground so sly,
"Did you hear what happened? Oh my!"

Mysteries twirl in fragrant air,
Can you sense the plants' wild dare?
With every scent, a joke unfolds,
In this world of greens and golds!

Secrets in the Garden

In the garden, whispers play,
Petals giggle in sunny rays.
Worms wear shades, oh what a sight,
Bees buzz jokes till the fall of night.

Tadpoles gossip, quite a crew,
Sipping dew like morning brew.
Rabbits chuckle, they can't get lost,
As flowers bloom, they laugh at frost.

Dance of the Delicate

Flowers waltz in breezy cheer,
Move like dancers, oh so dear.
Ladybugs twirl with perfect flair,
Even the ants join in with care.

Hummingbirds hum a funny tune,
As petals sway beneath the moon.
Grasshoppers leap with comic style,
In this garden, watch them smile.

Portrait of a Blooming Heart

A heart that blooms, oh what a game,
With petals wide, it is never tame.
It paints the air in vivid hue,
And laughs at clouds that drift on through.

With thoughts as bright as morning sun,
This heart is stubborn, full of fun.
It tickles bees, makes them all grin,
In the garden, joy begins.

The Lament of Flora

Flora sighs, her petals droop,
She feels too much like a clammy soup.
A squirrel stole her sunny seat,
Now she's plotting a funny feat.

With weeds that laugh and poke their heads,
She'll have her day, despite her dreads.
A prankster breeze, it gives her cheer,
To swirl and twirl without a fear.

Beauty Intertwined

In the garden, blooms divine,
Petals giggle, sip of wine.
Bees in bow ties dance around,
Bumbling serenades abound.

Bright colors clash, a comic scene,
Daisies plotting, it's obscene.
Tulips snicker, quite the crew,
As violets blow kisses too.

Roses roll their eyes in jest,
While sunflowers play dress-up fest.
With laughter bright, they twist and twine,
Nature's humor is so fine.

The Unfurling of Dreams

A bud winks in morning light,
Stretching slowly, oh what a sight.
Whispers of a dream take flight,
As morning dew giggles in delight.

Leaves are flipping like a page,
Each unfolding brings on a stage.
Stars of nature, quite the rage,
They moonwalk on the garden's stage.

So many wishes wrapped in hue,
Forming jokes, a quirky crew.
Petals laugh, and nature beams,
In the rhythm of unfolding dreams.

Luminous Gardens

In the glow of silver beams,
Petals dance, igniting dreams.
Fireflies laugh, twinkle and tease,
A luminary laugh, garden's breeze.

Roses play tag with ladybugs,
Hiding 'neath the leafy rugs.
Sunset giggles, colors swirl,
As blooms intend to give a twirl.

Dahlias sport their fanciest wear,
While pansies giggle without a care.
Nature's stage is set tonight,
In luminous laughter, a joyful sight.

The Lavender's Lullaby

Lavender's lullaby drifts through,
Singing sweetly, just for you.
Herbal humor in the air,
As the bumblebee spins in flair.

Moths in monocles sip on tea,
Discussing fashion with the bee.
Petals plot a soirée bright,
Under the stars, such a sight.

Giggling blooms hum soft and low,
Tickling each other, just to show.
In the garden, sleep does abide,
With laughter's kiss as dreams collide.

Memories in Full Bloom

In a pot far too small, it grew with flair,
A flower with secrets, it didn't care.
It whispered sweet nothings to bees on the go,
While plotting a trip to the neighbor's window.

With roots that entwined like a slippery dance,
It laughed at the gardener's confused little glance.
'You think I'm a plant? Just a pretty old face!
I'm the queen of this garden, my throne's in this space.'

Elysian Fields of Green

In fields where the sunflowers wear silly hats,
Roses recite jokes and tease the old cats.
The daisies hold court with a laugh and a cheer,
While lilies throw shade, their petals sincere.

'You'll never believe what the tulips told me!'
Said a jolly lilac, all giggles with glee.
'Our friends in the garden throw quite the rave,
But watch out for thorns—those pricks can be brave!'

Petals in the Breeze

A soft breeze came by with a mischievous sound,
Sending petals to dance, oh what joy they found!
Each flutter and twist told a funny old tale,
Of gardens and gnomes who'd gotten so pale.

The daisies kept spinning, 'Oh, look, it's a ghost!'
'No, silly,' said tulips, 'it's just that guy post!'
With laughter they twirled, made the sunbeam shine,
A parade of hilarity, sipping on twine.

The Beauty of Transience

As petals drop down like confetti in fall,
They giggle and flutter, 'We've had quite a ball!'
'We'll be back next year with new jokes to share,
So save us some sunshine, and always beware!'

For time may be fleeting, but oh, what a show,
The flowers remind us—it's fun to let go.
Embrace every moment, let laughter consume,
In the garden of joy, there's always more room.

Portraits of the Quiet

In a corner, petals sway,
Pretending it's a sunny day.
Folk stroll by, they stop and stare,
A flower posing, without a care.

Bumblebees, the paparazzi buzz,
Shooting selfies, just because.
With sticky fingers, they create,
A masterpiece of floral fate.

Each bloom a quirky, laughing face,
Making sure they own the space.
Quiet, but with a cheeky grin,
Whispers of the garden's din.

So here's to all the floral jest,
In their vivid, silly fest.
A portrait rich in silent glee,
Nature's art, wild and carefree.

Serenity in Each Stem

There's calmness in each leafy twist,
Yet frogs in tuxedos can't resist.
They hop around with flair and zest,
Sipping nectar like it's the best.

A ladybug brings tales of woe,
Of missed chances and a toe-to-toe.
But who can sulk with such fine views,
In gardens filled with laughter's hues?

The sun tickles, and the shadows dance,
While petals giggle, given the chance.
In every stem a poke, a tease,
A gentle joke swaying in the breeze.

So raise a toast to nature's jest,
In this serene, leafy fest.
For even in quiet, we find delight,
A world of whimsy, pure and bright.

A Garden of Quietude

In a garden where silence sings,
Daisies jest with imaginary kings.
Even the wind has a playful tone,
Whispering jokes in a language unknown.

A squirrel's hubbub, a sudden shout,
Makes all the blooms stand up and pout.
They quiver and giggle, a leafy crew,
Daring each other to dance anew.

Willow branches perform a show,
Teasing buds in giggly flow.
Nature's quiet, a loud disguise,
Where humor flourishes and never dies.

So if you stroll through this flowery maze,
Expect some laughter, in myriad ways.
For in this hush, a jest abounds,
A garden's giggle in tranquil sounds.

Hues of Harmony

Colors clash and hues collide,
In this garden, where all reside.
Roses blush, but tulips tease,
Creating chaos with delightful ease.

Violets gossip, nodding along,
While geraniums hum a cheery song.
They prank each other with gentle flair,
A mix of laughter fills the air.

The daisies munch on giggles bright,
While sunflowers show off their height.
In every shade, a tale unfolds,
A dance of whispers, bold yet coy.

So come and join this vibrant spree,
Where every leaf is wild and free.
In hues of harmony, we find joy,
Nature's laughter, nothing to annoy.

Against the Noise of Thorns

In a garden full of fuss,
The flowers shout and make a fuss.
Yet here I stand, a quiet bloom,
Dodging whispers, dodging gloom.

The bees all buzz and dance about,
While I just pout, my petals out.
They poke and jab, it's quite absurd,
I sigh and listen, it's my word.

A thorny joke they can't resist,
But I just pose, and coexist.
With petals soft as gentle jokes,
I laugh at all those noisy blokes.

So while they clash and scrabble round,
In silence, I am glory-bound.
With humor tucked in every leaf,
I bloom with joy, not bickering grief.

The Lullaby of Fragile Beauty

A fragile petal on the dance,
I sway to whispers, take a chance.
The breeze it tickles, makes me giggle,
While clumsy bugs just want to wiggle.

I see them stumble, trip and fall,
A dance-off happening, what a brawl!
With laughter bursting, oh so free,
I keep my calm, a sight to see.

As clouds above all make a fuss,
I stretch on down, no need to rush.
A lullaby hums sweet and clear,
With every rustle, life is dear.

So let the world be full of jest,
With silly dances, I feel blessed.
In fragile beauty, humor glows,
I bloom with joy where laughter flows.

Veils of Velvet and Dew

In velvet shades, I wrap my charm,
A sparkle here, a twist of arm.
The dewdrops giggle, bounce on down,
As I don my fancy jeweled crown.

A moth with dreams in wild pursuit,
Flops into me, oh, what a hoot!
I chuckle soft, 'You're quite the sight!
Like me, dear insect, take a flight!'

Each droplet weeps, but not in woe,
They join my dress for quite the show.
A drippy dance, a silly tease,
With glistening laughter in the breeze.

So if you wander past my way,
Join in the jest, come out and play.
In veils of velvet, joy's the cue,
A fun parade with me and you!

Grace in the Quiet Sun

When morning wakes with gentle grace,
I frolic slow in this warm place.
With sunlight tickling every part,
I beam the day, a happy art.

The ants beneath hold tiny wars,
While I just watch from leafy floors.
They march in line, a comic plight,
I shake my head, what a silly sight!

In gentle whispers, petals sway,
I laugh and giggle through the day.
With sunlit beams and playful vibes,
I dance along with nature's jibes.

So come, dear friend, and join the fun,
Beneath the rays of quiet sun.
In every bloom, a humor spun,
With grace and laughter, all is one.

Illuminated Twilight

In twilight's glow, a flower peeks,
Wearing a crown of purple cheeks.
She dreams of bees with dance so bold,
Yet fears the sun, that's far too gold.

With every tick, the petals twirl,
She sways and spins, a dizzy swirl.
A breeze arrives, and off she goes,
Chasing her shadow, striking a pose.

But wait! A squirrel, with nuts galore,
Tries to impress and knocks on the floor.
The flower giggles, what a sight!
Who knew a nut could cause such fright?

At last, the moon joins in the fun,
Painting the laughs till the night is done.
In this garden filled with glee,
The flower's antics bring joy to me.

The Gentle Heart of Nature

The petals dance, a waltz so sweet,
A ladybug joins with tiny feet.
She twirls and spins, a joyous jest,
While nature chuckles, feeling blessed.

A raindrop falls, a sudden blip,
And causes quite the sodden trip.
"Oh dear!" the flower starts to pout,
But here comes sunshine, clearing doubt.

With each new sun, her colors bloom,
She pops and giggles, chasing gloom.
"What a day!" she laughs with glee,
A flower's joy is wild and free.

Through gentle hearts of trees and grass,
She shares her tales; oh what a class!
In nature's realm, the mirth is rife,
For every bloom, there's a jest of life.

Ethereal Embrace

In the garden, where breezes play,
A flower dreams of a dance today.
With petals soft and a cheeky grin,
She invites the moon to spin and spin.

"Oh look!" she says, "A butterfly!"
"Let's twirl together, you and I!"
They flap and glide, a charming pair,
While giggling blooms just stop and stare.

But watch out for that sneaky snail,
Who thinks he's quick, yet leaves a trail.
The flower laughs as he trips and slides,
"Nature's dance truly has wild rides!"

In this embrace of moonlit play,
Joy twirls on each and every fray.
For in a garden, laughter glows,
Where every whimsy tends to grow.

Harmony in the Helix

In spirals bright, the petals shout,
"Join our party, there's no doubt!"
With every twist, the laughter spreads,
As pollen bounces on flower beds.

A bumblebee sets off to sing,
Yet finds himself caught mid-flower bling.
"Excuse me!" he buzzes, quite bemused,
In floral garb, he feels confused.

"Let's mix and mingle, give it a spin!
Nature's giggles, let the fun begin!"
The flowers chant, in harmony rare,
While grasshoppers dance without a care.

In this helix of joyful delight,
There's always a friend to brighten the night.
With petals prancing, a merry troop,
Nature's joy is one big goopy scoop.

Nature's Gentle Requiem

In the garden where whispers roam,
Petals giggle, feel right at home.
Bees and blooms in a silly race,
Wobbling chaotically, what a sight!

Leaves in chatter, banter so bold,
Telling tales of the sun's warm gold.
Roots are rumbling, what's for lunch?
A feast of dew? Oh, how they munch!

A butterfly pratfall, didn't see,
Landing smack dab on a bumblebee.
The flowers chuckle, oh what a scene,
Nature's shenanigans, always so keen!

So raise your teacup, let's cheer and toast,
To blooms and buzzes that thrill us the most.
With colors so bright, life's joyous swirl,
Nature's laughter, our happy world!

Dreams Woven in Stem

In a dreamy garden, where petals converse,
Stems spin stories, oh, they immerse.
A dandelion wearing a flower hat,
Telling tall tales of a brave chitchat!

The sunflowers stand, trying to strut,
Offering all the bees a free cut.
"Buzz on over!" they call with glee,
"We'll throw a party, just wait and see!"

Daisy heads bounce to a funky beat,
While tulips sway to the rhythm, oh sweet!
With each light breeze, they shimmy and sway,
In this floral fiesta, come join the play!

So laugh with the daisies, giggle with grass,
In this colorful dance, let worries pass.
With dreams woven tight in petals and stem,
Nature's delight, a joyous anthem!

The Allure of Delicate Shades

In hues of pink, yellow, and green,
Petals parade, a delicate scene.
"Who donned the blue?!" a flower shouts,
"Stop all the fuss! Let's sort this out!"

A rose winks, with a blush so bright,
"I borrowed the shade from the moon last night!"
Violets snicker, they can't help but tease,
"We're the cool kids, always a breeze!"

The pansies giggle, sharing their flair,
"Fashion's a bloom with a spring in the air!"
With colors and sparkles, they proudly convey,
"Join the fun, let's paint the whole day!"

Each petal twirls in a vibrant dance,
Floral giggles sprouting with every glance.
A palette unveiled beneath the sun's gaze,
Nature's laughter in delicate shades.

A Dance of Time and Light

As sunlight kisses the petals anew,
They frolic and giggle, it's quite the view.
Time joins the dance with a playful spin,
Tick-tock, they twirl; let the fun begin!

Morning dew drops play hide and seek,
While shadows cha-cha along the creek.
A squirrel leaps in, makes quite the fuss,
"Is this a party? Oh, count me plus!"

Old trees chuckle at the frolic below,
With stories of yesteryear, they steal the show.
"Once upon a time, oh what a sight,
A dance of the seasons, pure delight!"

So let's join the revelry of day and night,
In gardens where whimsy takes flight.
With laughter and joy, we'll greet the dawn,
In this whimsical world, let's dance on and on!

Garden of Whispers

In the garden, plants unite,
Talking gossip, what a sight!
Petals giggle, leaves all sway,
Birds eavesdrop on what they say.

Sun shines bright, the bees all hum,
While morning glories start to come.
A daisy winks, a rose pretends,
They're all just friends who twist and bend.

The tulips trade their sassy tales,
While daisies dance in sunny gales.
"Did you hear that?!" they squeal with glee,
As laughter floats from tree to tree.

With every breeze, they share a laugh,
Their joy a part of nature's craft.
In this garden, humor grows,
Where love and laughter freely flows.

Celestial Blooms

Up in the sky, with comets zoom,
Galaxies burst with bright, bold bloom.
Stars giggle as they twinkle bright,
Meteors dance in cosmic light.

A planet plots its flower show,
While moons make jokes that steal the glow.
Petunias in space take a sprout,
And sprinkle jokes, there's no doubt!

Comets wake with morning cheer,
"Did you hear the one about the sphere?"
A cactus wishes to join the fray,
But finds it hard to roll away!

As planets spin and galaxies sway,
They share their laughs in a playful way.
In the vastness, blooms align,
With every giggle, they intertwine.

The Allure of Vines

Twisting and turning, in a silly trance,
Vines wrap around, they love to dance.
A cheeky climb, a playful bound,
Tangled laughter, fun abound.

In the sunlight, they climb and sway,
Whispering secrets in a viney way.
"Hold my leaf, I've got a plan!"
Said the ivy to the innocent fern.

A sunflower watches with a smile,
As tulips agree with their own style.
"Let's make a crown! Let's trick the bee!"
They plot with glee, in jubilee.

Their games of twist, it's such a sight,
In the garden crown, all is right.
A tangle of fun among the green,
In this place, humor reigns supreme.

Secrets of the Serene

In calm waters where lilies float,
Swans are whispering, take note!
With feathered friends, they share their thoughts,
On what a frog truly wants.

A turtle laughs at the serpent's joke,
While catfish plot to tickle the oak.
"Do you think lilies can really fly?"
The pond ripples, and swans reply.

With every splash, they start to sing,
The water's humor, a lively spring.
"Let's have a party!" a frog decrees,
And everyone cheers with croaks and wheeze.

In these serene waters where laughter's sound,
The joy of nature is truly found.
Each creature shares their gossip thrill,
In this tranquil place, hearts are fulfilled.

Echoes from a Hidden Garden

In the garden of giggles, I sprout so bright,
Dancing with daisies, what a silly sight.
The bees buzz a tune, they can't hold a note,
While butterflies laugh as they play with my coat.

Worms tell the jokes that they've buried in dirt,
I snicker and wiggle, but it's hard not to spurt.
The laughter erupts, near the tulips, oh dear,
Even the sunflowers turn red with a cheer.

Rabbits hop by with their ears in a twist,
Chasing the sunlight, oh how can I resist?
The breeze plays along with its tickly touch,
While I bloom in bright colors, just laughing too much!

The daisies declare, "Let's have fun all day!"
And I, in my splendor, can't help but display.
Each petal's a giggle, each leaf's in a fit,
In this hidden garden, where humor's the hit!

Symphony of Colors Unfurled

A riot of colors in the morning sun,
Each petal a voice, oh what fun has begun.
Pansies are prancing, violets are wise,
While chattering roses wear glasses, no lies!

Day lilies sing out in a comical tune,
Snapdragons snap, such a silly festoon.
Hyacinths giggle, they can't keep it straight,
Their scents throw confetti, they celebrate fate!

Daffodils dance like they're lost in a dream,
While tulips compare just how tall they can beam.
A bumblebee joins with a stingy ballet,
And laughingly hums as it sways on its way.

As petals proclaim, let's party and cheer,
This riot of laughter we hold oh so dear.
In gardens of color, where giggles cascade,
The symphony blooms, a bright masquerade!

The Tapestry of Nature's Art

In a canvas of green where the colors collide,
Each petal a painting, a joy to abide.
The ivy is giggling; it tickles the fence,
While daisies poke fun just to fluster the tense.

A painterly world where the bees take the lead,
Mixing up colors with such zest and speed.
The sun sets ablaze, all the critters play fair,
As birdies compose tunes that float through the air.

The art of the garden, oh what a delight,
With sunflowers posing, they're ready to fight!
They challenge the tulips to a dance-off parade,
While violets chuckle, "We'll help you get laid!"

Flora and fauna, a whimsical crew,
Creating a laughter that's bright and so new.
In this tapestry woven with threads of pure mirth,
Nature's own comedy, a cherished rebirth!

Embrace of the Morning Light

The morning light giggles, it paints me in cheer,
Waking up flowers, they stretch, not a fear.
With yawns from the crocus, the tulips unwind,
Laughing at shadows, they're playful and kind.

The sunflowers pose for their selfies with glee,
While chatterbox blooms take their turns in the spree.
The daffodils joke, "Let's embrace the day!"
As colors collide in a whimsical play.

Butterflies flutter with stars in their eyes,
While hummingbirds zip like they're winning a prize.
The daisies join in, all decked out in flair,
Wiggling with joy, revelling in the air!

Oh, what a bright morn filled with warmth and delight,
With laughter unfurling, the world feels so right.
In this vibrant embrace soaked in giggly light,
Nature's own humor brings smiles to the sight!

In the Shade of Grace

In a garden where giggles bloom,
Petals dance to a floral tune.
With sun hats tilted, bees make a fuss,
Pollinating flowers, creating a buzz.

Ladybugs laugh in spots so bright,
Chasing each other in playful flight.
Daisies poke fun, in their daisy ways,
While shady grace brings lazy days.

A butterfly flits, with style and flair,
Wings like a cape, oh, who wouldn't stare?
With flirtatious moves, it twirls around,
While nature's laughter is the only sound.

So, beneath the leaves, join the delight,
As blossoms bring smiles from morning till night.
In this garden of giggles, come take your place,
In the shade of the flowers, let laughter embrace.

Threads of Silk and Sun

In sunlight's weave, flowers sway,
Spinning laughter in the play.
Silk threads of colors, a comical sight,
Dressing up petals, oh what a fright!

With spiders crafting webs of fun,
Their houses sparkle, catching the sun.
They invite everyone for a funny show,
Where even the plants put on a glow!

The daisies gossip, petals ajar,
Comparing their outfits, raising the bar.
"I'd match with the tulips, but not with the rose!"
And giggles erupt in floral prose.

So let's toast to blooms in styles so bright,
Where nature's humor shines with delight.
In threads of silk and sunlit spree,
Laughter's the flower that sets us free!

The Language of Lavender

In fields of lavender, whispers arise,
Secrets are traded, under clear skies.
These blooms speak softly, with hints of charm,
Beware of their winks, they mean no harm!

Lavender jokes, with humor so sweet,
Make all the bees dance and tap their feet.
With each petal giggle, the sun starts to glow,
As bees drop their pollen like confetti in slow.

Crickets join in with tunes so spry,
A symphony of chuckles in the sky.
As lavender sways, it knows what to say,
Laughter is the language that brightens the day!

So wander through fields where lavender waits,
With jokes and laughter, it never abates.
Let's speak in petals through giggles and grins,
In the language of blooms, everyone wins!

Echoes in the Greenhouse

In the greenhouse where echoes play,
Plants share stories in their own way.
A fern cracks jokes, with fronds so wide,
And in the corners, giggles reside.

Tomatoes blush with tales of delight,
As cucumbers chuckle all through the night.
While pots of herbs sing a spicy tune,
And dance like no one's watching, just under the moon.

The spider plant jokes, in quirky sass,
"I'm just hanging out; that's all I ask!"
Basil rolls its leaves, with laughter it's rife,
In this lively hub, plants celebrate life.

So come to the greenhouse, and join in the fun,
Where echoes of laughter unite everyone.
With leaves all abuzz in joyful embrace,
A world of humor, in this green place!

In Search of the Sublime

In the garden I roam, so bold,
Chatting with flowers, stories told.
A rose said, "I'm the Queen, you see!"
I laughed, "Oh please, just let it be!"

Sunlight glints on petals bright,
Yet bees buzz by, oh what a fright!
"Don't mind me!" they seem to declare,
With pollen humor, light as air.

The tulips giggle, swaying by,
While daisies play a little shy.
A sunflower winks, returns the jest,
In this floral world, I'm truly blessed.

Yet peeking closer, what do I spy?
A dandelion, raised up high!
"I'm more than fluff!" it boldly beams,
"Sowing laughter in your dreams!"

Strokes of Nature's Brush

Nature's artist, brush in hand,
Painting blooms across the land.
"Oh darling!" said a violet so fine,
"Your smile should be on canvas divine!"

With splashes of colors, bright and bold,
The lilies giggle, stories unfold.
"You think you're special?" a tulip teases,
While petals dance in playful breezes.

The poppies laugh, as red as fire,
Creating chaos, building desire.
"We bloom in fields! The best of spots!"
In their flirtatious banter, time rots.

Amidst this bloom, my heart does sway,
In this vibrant world, plants know play.
With strokes so wild, and voices sweet,
Each flower claims its dancing feat.

A Dance with the Divine

Beneath the sun, a flower's waltz,
With petals swirling, no faults.
"Step with me!" calls out the fern,
In this duet, we twist and turn.

The daisies stomp their little feet,
As fragrant sighs greet the beat.
A violet shimmies, catches gaze,
In this ballet, we're not in a haze.

But wait! Who twirls so out of place?
A dandelion, with no grace:
"I'm fluffy but fun, let's make a scene!"
And off it goes, in a puff of green.

We laugh and dance from day to night,
Nature's rhythm feels just right.
With every sway, a spark we find,
A joyous jig, so intertwined.

The Poetry of Petals

In the meadows, petals speak,
With whispers soft, just like a cheek.
"Roses are red," the blooms do rhyme,
While daisies tickle with silly chime.

"I'm not just pretty! I've got feels!"
A tulip shouts, with thrifty heels.
"I smell and shine, but also sway,
Tell me your petals, have their say?"

The lilacs brood, all purpled right,
"Life's just a poem, take a bite!"
Each petal tells a tale unique,
In this flowery realm, it's joy I seek.

Then down below, the grass takes stage,
"We're the base of this wild page!"
With laughter and blooms, oh, what a view,
In this garden, every word rings true.

Veils of Velvet and Dew

In gardens where the wild things play,
A bloom in pink just stole the day.
It quips and giggles in the breeze,
While laughing bees fly with such ease.

With velvet cloaks, she twirls about,
Whispers secrets without a doubt.
Sipping nectar, feeling spry,
While setting sun waves her goodbye.

The ants parade in perfect line,
Marching past, they think they're fine.
It's silly how the petals dance,
Creating chaos, given a chance.

So here's to petals, bright and bold,
In nature's tales, they're never told.
With every twist, a smile grows,
In this garden where laughter flows.

Radiant Solitude

In a pot by the window, so bright,
Sits a flower, ready for flight.
She winks at the sun with flair,
Sipping rain like it's a fair.

"Hello there, moth," she shouts with glee,
"Come dance with me, oh can't you see?"
With laughter shared on gentle nights,
They dream of strange, aerial flights.

Her petals stretch, a vibrant sight,
Waving at clouds in pure delight.
While bugs all giggle, putting on shows,
In her own world, nobody knows.

So here's to blooms that shine so bright,
With giggles trapped in morning light.
They hold their secrets, hiding well,
In radiant rooms where stories dwell.

Beneath the Canopy of Dreams

Underneath leaves, in a cozy nook,
A tiny flower opens its book.
With tales of giggles and breeze's delight,
She dreams of stars that twinkle at night.

The raindrops tap like a playful tune,
While spiders weave webs by the light of the moon.
"I'll spin a story, come gather near,
Of wise old frogs who sip on beer!"

Her petals wave, inviting all,
"Come join my gathering, we'll have a ball!"
Laughter bounces through the trees,
As fireflies join in with unearthed keys.

So here in dreams, let laughter bloom,
With petals wrapped in silly perfume.
In this secret spot, free of care,
Joy dances lightly in the air.

The Pulse of Petals

On a sunny day, a flower exclaims,
"I have the best of all the games!"
With petals flicking, she starts to prance,
Challenging shadows to join her dance.

The bumblebees buzz, "We're here to play!"
"Come on, let's sparkle, hip hip hooray!"
With every flutter, the laughter grows,
As bunnies hop in their Sunday clothes.

A breeze joins in, with a chuckle or two,
"Don't mind me, just passing through!"
Together they spin, the world a blur,
Petals and giggles, oh how they stir!

So here's to petals with spirits so bold,
In the warmth of laughter, life is gold.
Each moment shared, a sweet little thrill,
In gardens where giggles and petals are still.

Whimsy Among the Vines

A lady in purple, proud and bright,
She dances with bees, oh what a sight!
Her petals like skirts, twirling in glee,
Winking at bugs, come sip cup of tea.

Frogs tease and croak, with a jazz in the air,
While snails move their way, without a care.
"Race me, dear snail!" she giggles with flair,
But the snail just sighs, "I'm going nowhere!"

Meanwhile, the sun takes a bath in the lake,
As bluebirds sing songs, for goodness' sake!
The chair by the flowers, a comfy retreat,
But with pollen around, who can take a seat?

Yet laughter ensues, in this garden so grand,
As critters convene for a dance, hand in hand.
With petals and giggles, what more could there be?
In this vine-laden world, we just love to be free!

Echoes of Nature's Palette

In a field of colors, oh what a scene,
A sunflower gossiping with a vibrant green.
"Did you hear?" she asks, eyes wide with thrill,
"That tulip's been bragging, oh what a pill!"

The daisies chuckle, their heads bobbing slow,
While the lilies conspire, hiding their glow.
"Shall we put on a show, just for pure fun?"
"Yes! Let's have a laugh, 'til the day's done!"

A butterfly floats, with a mask on its face,
"I'm here for the drama, let's pick up the pace!"
The petals are clapping, they're ready to cheer,
Nature's wild party, we hold oh so dear.

Like paint on a canvas, dripping with joy,
The blooms on the branches, each girl and boy,
Echo the laughter that dances on breeze,
In this riot of color, let's all just tease!

Resonance of the Rare

One day in the meadow, a sight quite bizarre,
A flower with glasses gazes at a star.
"Oh look! A comet!" she shouts with delight,
"I'll name it my cousin, he's such a bright light!"

The postman is busy, delivering zest,
To the violets waiting, they're dressed to impress.
"Ill have a pink hat!" the geranium squeals,
"But not any blue one, that's not how it feels!"

Then comes a grasshopper, leaping about,
"What's that in your hair? Oh, it's just a doubt!"
"A doubt?" cries the violet, "How do they taste?"
"Like sweetness dipped chaos, come have with no haste!"

In this quirky garden, we giggle and prance,
Trading tall tales as we spin in our dance.
From flouncy to funny, each bloom has its flair,
In this garden of laughter, the world seems more rare!

A Caress of Color

In the garden, bright and bold,
Petals dance like stories told.
Colors waltz with sunny glee,
Whispering secrets to the bee.

With a wink of purple flair,
Even bugs stop, take a stare.
A splash of pink, a hint of blue,
They giggle, 'What more can we do?'

Laughter hides beneath each leaf,
A silent joke, a leafy thief.
Who knew that greens could jest?
With every breeze, they pass the test.

Oh, the sun is quite the tease,
He tickles petals with a breeze.
In radiant suits, they strike a pose,
Ignoring all who dare to doze.

The Enchanted Flora

In a world where flowers chuckle,
Dancing vines in playful buckle.
Each bloom wears a grin so wide,
Contemplating life's tomato slide.

Petal parties, oh what fun!
Where all the plants outshine the sun.
A daisy jokes with laughter bright,
Telling tales in morning light.

The tulips tease the old oak tree,
Mocking his lack of flexibility!
While daffodils play hide and seek,
In a game that's far from bleak.

Look at that stem, it wears a hat,
Fashioned from leaves, how about that?
With stripes of green and dots of gold,
A runway show in nature's mold.

The Mirth of Buds

Little buds with dreams so grand,
Busting out to take a stand.
With whispers that make squirrels laugh,
Imitating a photograph.

Soon they bloom, they're in the zone,
Chatting up the bees on loan.
Petals sashay, making friends,
Life's a party that never ends!

Frolicking under sunshine's grin,
Revelry is where it begins.
Wobbling shadows, tickled bright,
Even worms know how to delight.

In this crazy floral team,
Every color pairs like a dream.
A burst of laughter, sweet and pure,
Who knew plants could have such allure?

A Celebration in Bloom

Raise your glasses, flowers cheer,
Pollen party, the time is here!
Every hue and shade's invited,
Giggles erupt as buds are excited.

With glittering dew as their drink,
They toast to petals, not to shrink.
Violet laughs, and yellows sing,
This garden party's quite the thing!

Lilies tease with elegant flair,
Sharing tales of fragrant air.
Meanwhile, roses strike a pose,
With thorns that keep the grumps on toes.

A chorus of cheer, oh what a sight,
Under the sun, everything's bright.
Who knew flora had such style?
Their laughter echoing for a while!

When Shadows Bloom

In twilight's glow, they dance and sway,
Whispering secrets, in a playful way.
With petals bright, they tease the night,
Twirling round, a comical sight.

Their colors clash, like hats askew,
Poking fun at the buzzing crew.
"Why so serious?" one blooms loud,
As laughter rings through the flower crowd.

A bumblebee trips, takes a dive,
While petals chuckle, oh how they thrive!
With every bloom, a jest in view,
Nature's punchlines, fresh as the dew.

So join the frolic, let humor rise,
In gardens where laughter never dies.
For shadows bloom, with giggles and cheer,
In this quirky world, we hold so dear.

A Fragrant Reverie

A whiff of fun, in the garden today,
Flowers jesting, in their fragrant way.
"Do I smell bad?" a daisy will say,
While tulips giggle, and sway in dismay.

The roses blush, when the sun draws near,
"Who wore it best?" they jest without fear.
Lavender whispers, with laughter so light,
"Why be serious? Let's party tonight!"

Butterflies flutter, in comical grace,
Landing on petals, oh what a chase!
With colors so bright, it's a silly affair,
They flutter and giggle, without a care.

So join in the fun, as blossoms unite,
In this fragrant dream, let's dance with delight.
For every bloom holds a chuckle or cheer,
Making life brighter, all through the year.

The Dreamweaver's Garden

In a garden of dreams, where giggles abound,
   Petals are scheming, making joy sound.
  "What's the punchline?" a lily will ask,
    While daisies cackle, loving the task.

With each little breeze, they sway side to side,
   While shy violets watch, trying to hide.
A quirky old gnome, with a hat much too tall,
   Selfies with daffodils, giggling for all.

The moonlight chuckles, as stars take a peek,
At these cheeky blooms, oh how they speak!
In the hush of the night, their laughter's a tune,
   Comedic delights, like a cartoon balloon.

So come, take a stroll, in this playful domain,
Where flowers are jokers, and joy is the gain.
With dreams that are woven in colors so bold,
In the dreamweaver's garden, laughter is gold.

Flourish of the Tender

Oh, tender blooms with laughter to share,
Beneath sunshine's gaze, they dance without care.
"Why so floppy?" a petunia will chirp,
While sunflowers grin, doing a flip with a burp!

With giggles and snorts, they sway in the heat,
Telling tall tales, oh what a treat!
A petal's a wig, and a leaf's a small hat,
For merriment's sake, they're loving all that!

Through puddles they leap, in a bold little style,
Mud on their faces, but full of a smile.
Bumblebees buzzing, with rhymes in their hum,
"Join us, dear friend, let's all be a drum!"

So dance in the garden, with joy in your step,
For love blooms in laughter, in every rep.
In this flourish of tender, let whimsy take flight,
Where humor's the bloom that blossoms each night.

Whispers of the Petal

In a garden, I heard a shout,
'You can't be serious, what's this about?'
A flower giggled, swayed side to side,
'I'm the most fabulous, can't you abide?'

The daisies chuckled, the roses sighed,
'Look at that bloom, so full of pride!'
With every breeze, it flaunted its flair,
'I'm the queen here, no need to compare!'

A bee buzzed near, with laughter so sweet,
'You think you're the best? Well, isn't that neat!'
In the floral court, a spectacle grand,
Each petal a player, oh, don't you understand?

They whispered secrets, each tale a delight,
Of pollen parties that last through the night.
With every joke, the garden would bloom,
Laughter and petals—an eternal perfume.

Dances in the Shade

Under the leaves, a party unfolds,
With flowers and ferns, the tale is retold.
A sunflower twirled, with a goofy grin,
'Can you believe the mess that I'm in?'

A daffodil stammered, tripped on a root,
'I'm not meant for dancing, just look at my suit!'
But the host was a lilac, bright and spry,
'Just let loose a little, forget the why!'

They waltzed and they spun, amidst giggles and glee,
The dandelions joined, as wild as can be.
With each little flap and flutter, they laughed,
In the shade, where the sunlight was daft.

Then came a breeze, with its cheeky command,
'Time to shake things up, oh isn't it grand?'
The flowers burst out, in a riot of cheer,
In the sanctuary of green, joy went rogue here.

Elegance in Bloom

In the morning light, with a nod and a wink,
A flower posed, on the brink of a pink.
With petals so fancy, it struck a fine pose,
'If beauty were a battle, I'd win it, who knows?'

A bee whispered softly, 'You think you're the best?'
An insect parade was put to the test.
'You're lovely, dear bloom, but can you do tricks?'
With a dramatic sigh, it exclaimed, 'What a fix!'

The tulips were snickering, thanks to the breeze,
'Catch her if you can, with such gentle ease!'
So the flower pirouetted, not one petal lost,
Strutting its stuff, at whatever the cost.

A ladybug chimed in, 'Why not share the fame?'
But the elegant blossom just flaunted its name.
'Let's make the garden a runway, my dears!'
And so, they all twirled, casting off their fears.

Secrets of the Silken Stem

Down low, the wispy whispers do sneak,
A stem shared a story, that made all hearts peak.
'Have you seen the shrub? It thinks it's a tree!'
The giggles erupted, as loud as can be.

They laughed at the petals, how they blush and sway,
While grasses just trembled, in their humble display.
'We keep our cool, even in the sun's glare,'
The violets hummed, 'with style and with flair!'

Then came a night, with the moon's gentle gleam,
And the petals all danced, as if caught in a dream.
'What's the secret?' a bud poked, oh so bold,
'Just let laughter in, and you'll never grow old!'

So the garden reveled, beneath star-studded skies,
A bounty of laughter, with not one disguise.
In each whispering petal, and each silken thread,
Joy blossomed freely—laughter still spread.

Serene Breaths in Floral Silence

In a pot I sit all day,
My roots a tangled ballet.
Sunshine tickles my green leaves,
While dreaming of mischief and thieves.

The gardener thinks I'm quite sweet,
But I've schemes planned, oh so neat!
When no one's around, I will dance,
And mock all flowers with a glance.

Sometimes I feel like a diva,
Strutting like my name's on a visa.
With petals soft as whipped cream,
I reign over a floral dream.

So here's to me, the silent queen,
In this garden, I reign supreme.
With each breeze, I raise a toast,
To laughter, petals, and my ghost.

The Soul of a Sunlit Garden

In the sun, I stretch and yawn,
Plotting pranks from dusk till dawn.
The bees think I'm a lovely sight,
But I giggle when they take flight.

My neighbors boast of vibrant hues,
But I'm the one with laughter cues.
I tickle the daisies just for fun,
And prank the roses on the run.

With squirrel friends, we tell tall tales,
Of secret paths and treasure trails.
In this garden, full of cheer,
Every moment's worth a sneer!

So if you find a flower grinning,
You'll know it's me, the fun beginning.
In blossoms bright, let laughter bloom,
As nature chuckles in this room.

Captured in a Moment's Dawn

As the sun peeks over the fence,
I brew my jokes, a floral suspense.
The lilacs laugh, they know my game,
In morning's light, I'll stake my claim.

With morning dew, I start my schemes,
Creating laughter from wild dreams.
I tease the tulips, a playful jibe,
While bees do the work, I'll just vibe.

In this serene embrace of dawn,
The world wakes up, the fun goes on.
With petals fluttering like tales untold,
I'm the mischief-maker, bold and gold.

So here's to dawn, that playful light,
Where flowers join in sheer delight.
In this dance of colors and glee,
I'm the jester of this jubilee!

Lament of the Wandering Breeze

Oh breeze, you wander here and there,
Tickling petals, causing a stare.
I'd join your dance, but I'm too rooted,
This floral life I've long computed.

You carry jokes from flower to tree,
While I stand still, just sipping tea.
"Join us!" they call, but I demur,
My petals shake with a harmless stir.

You tease the lilies without a care,
While I commit to my grounded affair.
With every gust, you steal a grin,
But here, I'm stuck—oh where to begin?

If only I could join your spree,
I'd flip and flop quite joyfully.
But for now, I'll watch from my spot,
The breezy laughs, my favorite plot.

Blooming Memories

In the garden, a flower did tease,
Wearing colors that winked in the breeze.
Its petals were floppy, it danced with delight,
No one could miss it, a comical sight.

With blossoms like hats, it changed its attire,
It giggled with bees, buzzing ever so higher.
Each bloom a reminder of funny old tales,
Of mishaps in spring, and whimsical fails.

Through sun and through rain, it lightens the air,
Camera-ready moments, we stop and we stare.
It waves at the sun with its goofy green stem,
Inviting us in, it says, "Join my fun gem!"

So here's to the blooms that tickle our hearts,
With laughter and smiles, that's where happiness starts.
In our garden of giggles, let memories grow,
As we cherish these moments, let our joy overflow.

Soft Shadows of Beauty

In twilight's embrace, they sway and they sway,
Casting shadows that dance, in a cheeky ballet.
Petals draped low, oh what a surprise,
They fashion a cloak, of giggles and sighs.

With whispers of colors, they play peek-a-boo,
Like shy little sprites, they flit into view.
Beneath leafy canopies, they chuckle and cheer,
"Come watch us, dear friends! We've got laughter here!"

They juggle the sunlight, a trickster's delight,
With hues that blend softly, in the fading light.
They mimic the moon with their silvery gleam,
Inviting enchantment in every sweet dream.

So tiptoe in shadows, share smiles with the blooms,
For nature's comedians fill gardens with tunes.
In laughter and beauty, let joy bloom anew,
Embrace the soft shadows, they're waiting for you!

A Tapestry of Fragrance

In a riot of scents, where aromas collide,
A tapestry woven where dear friends abide.
Each whiff a giggle, a memory spry,
With notes of sweet chaos that float in the sky.

Lavenders laugh while the marigolds tease,
A fragrance buffet, oh what a breeze!
With sniffles and chuckles, we twirl through the air,
Spinning tales of friendships, with stories to share.

The fragrance of mischief wraps 'round like a shawl,
Whispers of laughter, the best gift of all.
Forget-me-nots chuckle, "Don't let this fade!"
As we linger in moments that memories made.

So take a deep breath and join the parade,
Of scented delights in the blooms that we grade.
With each silly whiff, let the joy help you roam,
In this fragrant delight, you'll find a new home.

The Gilded Stem

With a stem that shines bright, it struts with great flair,
Dripping in humor, it spins through the air.
Leafy companions all join in the fun,
Together they sparkle, like rays from the sun.

In the spotlight of laughter, they sway to the beat,
With petals of gold, they dance on their feet.
Chuckles are plenty, beneath moonlight's charm,
It smiles all around, oh what a calm balm!

The gilded one boasts, with a wink of its leaf,
"Without me, dear garden, you're missing the chief!"
It lifts up its voice, a comical jest,
In bloom with pure laughter, it truly's the best!

So treasure the stem, with its gilded display,
For laughter's the sunlight that brightens the way.
In gardens of glory, let joy be the theme,
And cherish the moments, like a sweet, silly dream.

A Symphony of Colors

In the garden, blooms so bright,
Colors clash, what a sight!
Yellow screams, while blue just hides,
Red says, "Hey! Let's take sides!"

Petals prance in a fun ballet,
Dancing around, come what may.
Green leaves snicker, think it's rude,
While petals tease, "Just change the mood!"

A bee gets lost in the swirl,
Buzzing loud, causing a whirl.
"Your color's nice, but what's the catch?"
Pollens laugh, a fine mismatch!

With flowers blushing, it's clear to see,
Nature's joke is quite the spree.
So many laughs in floral space,
Giggles bloom, oh what a place!

In the Embrace of Petals

In a world of vibrant spritz,
Petals hug, despite some splits.
A daisy said, "Do I smell?"
A rose replied, "No, it's just swell!"

Butterflies join, now what a mess,
Chasing scents, it's pure excess.
"I'm the best!" shouted one in flight,
While others rolled, a comical sight!

In sunlit spots they lay in glee,
Pets and blooms, a circus spree.
"What's that smell?" the tulips teased,
"Oh it's just Herb, always so pleased!"

Each bloom has its own strange quirk,
Silly tales in the floral work.
In their embrace, we find more laughs,
Nature's humor is a goodie stash!

The Soliloquy of Stems

Stems stand tall, a proud display,
"I hold it all!" they proudly say.
"But what's that odor? Not from me!"
A mess of petals, quite the spree!

Wobbly stems try to keep straight,
One tipped over, now isn't that fate?
"Hey, I'm solid!" they incorrect,
While laughing leaves give them respect.

From each stem, a tall tale spun,
Of holding weights, and stubborn fun.
"Who knew we'd be the center of jokes?"
While roses giggle and wink like folks!

In this stage of life and sway,
It's clear that stems have found their play.
With each quip shared, blooms take their chance,
To join the humor, and frolic in dance!

Reveries of the Rare

Rare blooms whisper tales at night,
Sharing secrets, oh what a sight!
"I'm exotic!" says one with flair,
While a simple bud gives a smirk and stare.

"You think you're grand with colors tight?"
A cactus chimed in, with pure delight.
Finding joy in their odd parade,
Making memories that won't soon fade.

Uniqueness woven in every thread,
Funny tales of what was said.
The rarest heart can make you grin,
With wisdom growing from deep within.

So let's all join this flowering show,
With laughter growing as gardens grow.
In the reverie of petals rare,
Life's a circus, come with flair!

Beneath the Whispering Trees

In the garden where whispers play,
Little blooms dance in the fray.
They wear hats made of dew,
Sipping sunlight, fancy and new.

A bumblebee takes a curious glance,
Tripping over the flowers' prance.
Petals giggle, "Look at him buzz!"
While chasing a sweet, floral fuzz.

The butterflies flaunt in vibrant show,
Practicing moves only flowers know.
A gust of wind laughs, sways the lot,
Nature's jesters in a sunny spot.

Under trees where secrets bloom,
They hide from the world, in floral room.
With silly faces, they sway and beam,
Living life like a joke or dream.

Petals in the Twilight

When daylight fades to a purple hue,
Petals gather 'round for a view.
They swap stories of the sun's bright prance,
And giggle at clouds that miss their chance.

A nocturnal critter joins their spree,
Wearing pajamas made from a tree.
The flowers chuckle, they can't resist,
As the raccoon dances with a twist!

Stars twinkle above with winks and grins,
While petals sway and join in spins.
Tonight's the night for laughter and cheer,
As moonlight whispers, "Don't hold back, dear!"

The night wraps them in a velvet hug,
As they share secrets, warm and snug.
With a comedic twist, they finish their songs,
In a world where flowers know they belong.

The Heart of Blooming Silence

Amidst the silence, flowers conspire,
To concoct a joke that'll rise higher.
They wait patiently for the moon's riddle,
To play hide and seek, oh what a middle!

A ladybug joins with a punny flair,
"Where do you hide when you need fresh air?"
The flowers snicker, their petals so light,
Making merry in the soft moonlight.

Crickets chirp in comedic tone,
As petals hum a joyful drone.
Each lullaby a tickle to hear,
Bringing giggles that softly appear.

In silence blooms, there's a playful tease,
Life's merriment sways in the breeze.
As laughter bursts from every seam,
They bloom with joy, embracing the dream.

Echoing Serenity

In the realm of sneaky twilight's grasp,
Blooms whisper secrets, time to unmask.
They giggle as shadows start to blend,
Sharing tales that never quite end.

A cheeky squirrel hops from tree to tree,
As flowers giggle, "Look at him flee!"
They play peek-a-boo with the fading light,
Giving each other an enviable fright.

The stars join in with a twinkle and wink,
While petals ponder, and pause to think.
"Why is the moon always such a tease?"
They chatter and chuckle, moving with ease.

In echoing serenity, they prance and play,
Finding joy in the night's ballet.
With every giggle and soft, gentle sway,
They celebrate dreams till the break of day.

A Tribute to the Unfurling Life

In a garden of giggles, I stand so bright,
Waving my petals in sheer delight.
With each morning stretch, I dance so wide,
Pollen in the air, oh what a ride!

Dewdrops bouncing on my leaves, oh dear,
I'm not just pretty; I bring the cheer!
Bees buzzing my tunes, they think I'm a star,
But I'm just a flower who's making it far!

The sun peeks over, what a sight to behold,
I pose like a model, gleaming, bold.
Yet, as I strut in the warm sun's embrace,
I trip on a petal, oh what a disgrace!

But I giggle and giggle, red-faced and shy,
Life's just a comedy, oh my!
Every bloom's a laugh, a story to tell,
In my leafy kingdom, all is well!

Petals Kissing the Morning Mist.

With the dawn comes a shiver, I stretch up high,
Whispering sweet nothings to the sky.
The mists tickle softly, a gentle embrace,
I'm giggling so much, I can't hold my place!

Look at me, I'm fluttering here and there,
Trying to impress a wandering hare.
"Do you see my colors? They shine so bright!"
But he just hops away, quite out of sight.

The morning mist hugs, oh what a game,
Making my petals parade like a name.
I'm caught in a breeze, I twirl and I spin,
As the little breeze laughs, "Let the fun begin!"

A dance in the garden, who could resist?
Nature's comedy show with a twist.
So here I bloom, a chuckle in air,
All alone in my beauty, but I don't care!

Whispers of Petals

In the cool of the evening, petals convene,
Sharing secrets of being serene.
"I saw a bug, oh what a sight!
He danced on my leaf, it gave me a fright!"

"Did you see that bee with a giggly buzz?
He's got all the moves, but no one loves."
We chuckle together, so lively and bold,
Plant gossip is better than stories of old!

The moon peeks in, "What's all this chat?"
"Can't sleep," say the blossoms, "we're too busy, that's that!"
"Let's plot our escape on this lazy night,
We'll dance in the starlight, what a delight!"

But then comes the night breeze, tossing us around,
And we giggle and sway without making a sound.
These whispers of petals, so soft in the dark,
Are simply a laughter, a splendid remark!

The Elegance of Blooms

Oh, behold the blooms, look how they prance,
Swaying in gardens, it's all a dance!
With colors so bright, like kids at play,
We're competing for laughter, day after day!

"Watch me shine, I'm the belle of the ball!"
"Not so fast," says a daisy, "I'm having a ball!"
Together we giggle, our petals in flight,
Who knew being elegant could be such a sight?

Here comes the wind, with a cheeky little shove,
We twirl and we tumble, a giggly shove.
"Oh dear, look at us, what a marvelous mess!"
With every mishap, we're grinning, no stress!

As night falls gently, the laughter subsides,
We gather our joy; oh, how it abides!
In the elegance of blooms, a silly sweet cheer,
For life is a dance, let's bloom without fear!

A Serenade in Stems

In a garden, I prance, with leaves so chic,
Tall and nice, not a stem too weak.
I wiggle and sway in the warm, soft air,
Strutting my stuff without a care.

With a wink to the bees, I say, "Come play!"
Buzzing around in a silly ballet.
Sunshine tickles my petals so bright,
Making me giggle with sheer delight.

The breeze starts to laugh, it twists and spins,
I dance like I'm livin' in a world of wins.
With every little gust, I sway and twirl,
Who says a flower can't rock and whirl?

So if you see me, stop and stare,
This little bloom has flair to spare.
In the garden of giggles, I'm the queen,
In my floral kingdom, I'm the lively scene.

Echoes of Elegance

In a pot of elegance, I stand so proud,
With roots that giggle beneath a soft shroud.
When the sun hits me just right, I gleam,
A posh little flower, living the dream.

I throw shade to the weeds with a toss of my hair,
"You're just grass! Go on, I swear!"
Every time the gardener comes to check,
I flaunt my petals; he's a total wreck.

I whisper to daisies, telling them jokes,
They snicker and sway, like frolicking folks.
With laughter in petals, we bloom all day,
In this garden of humor, we're here to play!

Oh, the world outside may seem quite drab,
But in floral fashion, we're a snazzy fab.
So join our gala, where laughter is pure,
In echoes of elegance, we dance and endure!

Luminous Blossoms Under Moonlight

When the moonbeams tickle the garden floor,
I glow like a star, who could ask for more?
Dancing shadows make me chuckle and cheer,
Under this moonlight, I'm the belle of the sphere!

Swaying with laughter, I woo the night air,
Crickets join in; it's a musical affair.
"Do you see my glamour?!" I tease the stars,
With petals aglow, I'm a flower in cars.

Even the owls can't help but laugh, so wise,
At my nightly antics beneath the skies.
Whispers of petals, oh what a delight,
In this luminous song, everything feels right!

So tiptoe through gardens where laughter blooms bright,
In moonlit moments, we're pure dynamite.
With giggles and glimmers, our beauty unfurls,
We're the hidden stars in this garden of curls.

The Heartbeat of Nature

In the rhythm of roots, hear the nature's beat,
Wiggle and giggle, this life is sweet.
With petals tapping out their shiny tune,
I'm the flower that dances all afternoon.

The sun gives a wink, and I toss my head,
"Watch me swirl 'round," I giggle instead.
Ladybugs tap-dance on my soft skirt,
Now that's what I call a fashionable flirt!

Nature's heartbeat echoes, a vibrant sound,
With chuckles and blooms all around.
In this wild ballet, all creatures unite,
Swaying together till morning's first light!

So join in the fun, come twirl and prance,
In the heartbeat of nature, you'll find your chance.
A garden of laughter, bright and alive,
Where every bloom knows how to thrive!

www.ingramcontent.com/pod-product-compliance
Lightning Source LLC
Chambersburg PA
CBHW070311120526
44590CB00017B/2630